Canon David Hewetson has ministered in a range of diverse contexts and among many different people over more than fifty years. He was ordained into the Anglican ministry in the Diocese of Sydney and initially served in suburban parishes. He then went to Tanganyika (now Tanzania) as a CMS missionary at the time when many African countries were demanding independence. Canon Hewetson was appointed Principal of St Philip's Theological College at Kongwa where he trained numerous candidates for the African ministry. On returning to Australia he continued to serve with CMS as its Education Secretary and later as NSW General Secretary. He is married to Ann and they have three married children and seven grandchildren. This is his ninth book.

Acknowledgements

All images and photos used in this book have been reproduced with permission of the copyright holders.

National Library of Australia Cataloguing-in-Publication entry

Author:	Hewetson, David, 1929–
Title:	Good for you : the extraordinary life of the ordinary Christian / David Hewetson.
ISBN:	9781921577147 (pbk.)
Subjects:	Christian life – Anglican authors.
Dewey Number:	248.483

Cover design, typesetting and layout by Graham Lindsay, Barton Books.

Published 2012 by

Barton Books, 15 Blackall Street, Barton ACT 2600 Australia.

ABN: 26 130 172 093

Email: info@bartonbooks.com.au

Printed and bound by KainosPrint.com.au
PO Box 311, Calwell ACT 2905

GOOD FOR YOU

The *extra*ordinary life of
the ordinary Christian

*For Betty a family
love from David*

David Hewetson

Barton Books
Canberra, Australia
2012

GOOD FOR YOU

Introduction

The origins of this little book are closely linked with my own personal spiritual journey. What I learned as a young preacher and later as a missionary were welded into my message and eventually solidified into the sixty pages that follow. My own story is uncomplicated. It started with a call to ministry and developed from basic theological education and a strong evangelical commitment to the common search for 'something more.'

I emerged from my theological education not entirely satisfied with either the Church I sought to serve or with myself as one who sought to be of service. Perhaps uncharitably I judged the local scene with a young man's intolerance and the over-confidence commonly found among those with little experience of life. If I had been more assured of my own spiritual state then perhaps my judgement might have been more realistic. I suspect this restlessness made me ripe for something extra; something that would not in any way diminish the evangelical orthodoxy I cherished. This 'something extra' came for me largely through the dynamic ministry of someone who was, like me, a fledgling Anglican minister: Geoffrey Bingham. He was a former soldier decorated for bravery whose outlook was forged in the crucible of the Changi Prison of War Camp in Singapore. In those testing circumstances he plumbed the depths of his spiritual life and found it necessary to re-examine the basics of Christian orthodoxy until God raised him to a more profound faith and a more expansive Christian commitment. In his subsequent parish ministry, Geoff was lead by God into a fuller understanding of the Biblical doctrine of the Christian life. These discoveries and how they shaped his ministry Geoff readily shared with others. I felt privileged to be among them.

As we met together to explore broader possibilities for Christian growth we soon recognised that spiritual 'additions' were not needed. What we did need was a better understanding of what we already possessed in Christ. This led us to a closer study of St Paul's doctrine of the Christian life especially its depiction in chapters 6 to 8 of his letter to the Romans. In some ways our discovery resembled the message of the 'Keswick Conventions' (which began in 1875 and concentrated on enhancing the spiritual life) and its focus on the essential nature of sin and the 'double' power of the cross to not only deal with guilt but with sin's power as well. We became radical realists especially when it came to expounding the sinfulness of human nature and its corrosive consequences. Some older evangelicals became rather anxious about our emphasis on these things, possibly thinking that our emphasis was little more than the re-emergence of the dangerous teaching on the possibility of achieving sinless perfection in this world. This teaching had devastated the lives of some of their Christian contemporaries and dispirited many others. We were quite confident, however, that this was not the case.

This new understanding of what we already possessed in Christ was liberating and life-changing. It seemed to lend new power to my proclamation of the Bible's message and it opened new opportunities for outreach and engagement. I was in demand to speak in churches or at church camps. With hindsight I may have accepted too many of these attractive invitations. One of my parish critics once said that a fitting title for me would be 'minister without portfolio!' Another part of the story of this period of my life – although this is not the place to tell it – was being assaulted by a severe bout of depression. I felt great delight in living the Christian life and preaching the Christian message but I was assailed by emotional despair and debilitated by feelings I could not explain. The depression did not stop me moving at a great pace but it restricted my progress in a way that later seemed to me a blessing because it became an important part of my spiritual development.

Members of our little 'revival movement' sponsored 'deeper life' conventions which morphed into missionary conventions like those still being held at Keswick (which also encouraged a call to deeper Christian living). The culminating message of these week long gatherings was an emphasis on Christian service, however demanding it might have seemed. It appeared that the call to some form of missionary service was a natural outcome of what we were teaching. It was hardly surprising when we were convicted by our own message and offered to serve overseas. Bingham led the way. He became a missionary in Pakistan.

With the passing of more than five decades I have learned some valuable lessons about revival movements and all that we said and did in those years. First, it appears impossible to enter into new spiritual experiences without somehow giving others the impression - even unintentionally - that they are not quite where you are. In effect, you have achieved greater progress and become more selfless along the way. In my zeal to explain the 'real truth' about the Christian life, sadly I lost a few friends. As time passed I was obliged to work hard to regain their goodwill. Second, our doctrine might not have been what it should have been. I remember Geoff writing to me from Pakistan with the fear that we had not been 'correct' in a particular aspect of our teaching. When I responded by asserting that we must have been right because God had blessed our efforts so richly, he replied with words that have always been for me a useful reminder when assessing revivals: 'God does not bless our muddled heads, he blesses our obedient hearts.' Zeal and exuberance must never be an excuse for promoting poor theology. But I took solace from the fact that in our frailty we 'see through a glass darkly' which means we nevertheless see the true light of all. What remains most dear to me now originated in those halcyon days. In this book I have tried to set down, albeit in outline form the treasures we discovered.

After Geoff offered himself for service in Pakistan, I applied to the Church Missionary Society for an overseas post. Put simply:

our strong missionary emphasis needed to be turned into action. My progress was hindered almost immediately by an inability to obtain a visa. I also changed my mind about where I felt called to serve. The delay benefited me in two significant ways. First, it provided the opportunity to meet and marry Ann! Second, it gave me the opportunity to clarify the essence of the message I hoped to share in a series of talks that forced me to be concise and coherent. How this came about is worth recounting.

The 1959 Billy Graham Crusade had had a significant impact on the city of Sydney and there were many new people in our churches. The Sydney diocesan synod felt that our department of evangelism – the Board of Diocesan Missions – should offer the churches teaching missions so as to explain and apply the Christian faith. Since I was waiting around for more explicit missionary orders they asked me to take on this challenging task. There followed some very exciting times as I moved from parish to parish teaching, answering questions, selling Christian books and talking with people about the imperatives of Christian living. I began to see how important it might be to record what I was teaching and by the time Ann and I left for Tanganyika (later Tanzania) the book was only half written. Getting to the mission field in those days took considerable time. It usually took five weeks from Sydney to Africa with a stopover in Bombay along the way. It gave me sufficient time to learn enough from the book *Teach Yourself Swahili* to read on a warehouse in Mombasa the words: 'Europeans must go'. This was a salutary message for this European who had just come! We had arrived, of course, on time to witness the emergence of the large number of independence movements in Africa. We saw the Union Jack lowered and the new flag raised. 'God Save the Queen' was sung for the last time. In its place was 'God bless Africa'.

To give our Swahili a chance to consolidate we completed two English-speaking chaplaincies which involved *safaris* to a gold mine, a diamond mine, a coffee farm and – in the company of an African pastor – to several sisal farms. Independence meant an abrupt end to many promising careers among those employed by the Colonial Service. It was a particularly anxious time for them as they returned to Britain not really knowing what they would do. At the Independence Day celebrations in Tanganyika the retiring District Commissioner, who was handing over to an African named Leonard, said to me: 'we had thought of having a truck in the parade with me sitting in an 'out' tray and Leonard in an 'in' tray'. Thankfully in Tanganyika the new era was achieved relatively peacefully. But racial tensions sometimes emerged. They were usually offset in churches by a spirit of Christian fellowship and fraternity.

In 1963 we proceeded to what we thought was our 'real' missionary work: the principalship of St Philip's Theological College at Kongwa. Perhaps the local bishop (the legendary Alfred Stanway) was taking a bit of a risk appointing a first-term missionary to such a significant post. But he was kind enough to say about my qualifications that 'there is no substitute for common sense'. I later referred to myself on occasion as 'the last of the amateurs'. My Swahili was, however, working pretty well and that was our main teaching medium. We offered a three-year course for those training for ordination in either the Anglican or the Moravian churches. During part of the course wives and children also came into residence. Since the students were from a number of different tribes there were interesting, sometimes volatile, interactions. Relationships were strained. As the Church in Tanzania had been profoundly influenced by the East African Revival Movement my early experience of 'revivalism' was of some help in understanding the Church's mood and creatively working within it. We fed our students through the College kitchen and Ann, as a trained nurse, ran a clinic. She also taught some practical household tasks to the women and worked – with regular morning teas – in oiling the relational wheels of our strong-minded staff. Two of our children were born in Africa. In 'living the Christian life' in this demanding setting, I finally had the material to finish the still unfinished book.

When we returned to Australia a long-standing medical condition afflicted Ann and, after some serious surgery, CMS decided that we should not return to Tanzania. I moved 'sideways' into working at the CMS headquarters initially as Education Secretary and then as General Secretary of the (NSW) State Branch. This gave me a deep love of the romantic missionary story but also the practical dynamics of missionary endeavour. I decided to concentrate on the emerging discipline of missiology and this led to my appointment as the first (part-time) Head of the Department of Mission at Moore Theological College in Sydney.

And the book – what became of it? I brought the incomplete

manuscript back from Africa. It was re-written a number times. You have the finished form in your hands - the fruit of more than fifty years of reflection. I invite you to begin with the confident declaration by Mrs Springer (not her real name) about how to be 'good' and then come with me into the Bible to find out what being good means for a Christian. I trust that in reading the book it will also be 'good for you'.

David Hewetson
Sydney
Easter 2012

1   The Good Woman

Many years ago I was buying my first typewriter in a large Sydney department store. In those days, before easy credit – and credit cards – it was necessary to go to the Store's office to fill in the paper work after a purchase had been made. I found myself there sitting alongside a very erect lady who introduced herself as Mrs Springer. I introduced myself and explained that I was a fledgling minister working mostly with young people. 'Oh,' snorted Mrs Springer, 'the young people!' I got the immediate impression that she took a pretty dim view of the young and their general behaviour. I think that in their defence I probably, in so doing, suggested that we are all fallen creatures and in need of forgiveness. At this Mrs Springer became even more erect: 'we are all good' she exclaimed. I took it that she meant that she, and Mr Springer and all the little springers (if there were any) were models of good behaviour and apparently in no need of forgiveness.

I was so taken aback by her forthright declaration that I failed to say what – in retrospect – I wanted to say. I wanted to say that I too wanted to be a good person but I had discovered that the way to do this was probably very different to the way she was proposing. If we had had more time together I might have had a chance to offer the Bible's recipe for good living as something that emerges on the other side of a radical spiritual revolution. I might have shared with her that when we abandon our 'works' (self-effort) and apply to God for forgiveness he will then equip us for the 'good works' that he has in mind for us to do. I would have explained that this is how I had discovered the way to be a good man.

I suppose my dialogue with Mrs Springer still goes on in my mind and sometimes it asks the question: am I a *good* man and what kind of good man have I become? Am I simply a reasonably moral person but whose vaunted 'goodness' is nothing out of the ordinary. I thought of the little girl who prayed 'Lord, make all the bad people good and all the good people nice' and wondered whether she was thinking of those who claim by God's help to be living the right way but whose life style is not always very attractive. Is there somewhere – in the Bible for example – a description of believers who are good people but who have somehow missed the point? Is there also a way of discovering – also in the Bible – how to find the right way to be good in a manner that is engaging and attractive?

The very ordinary Christians

In the early church – in the city of Corinth - there was a remarkable group of Christians who had somehow become rather 'ordinary'.[1] Their very existence as a church was in itself a miracle. Corinth was a by-word in sexual immorality with a sordid life-style promoted by local pagan religion. But when St Paul visited them he saw how the power of the Gospel could blow people out of the moral mud heap, even though they still faced a variety of temptations. Added to their new Christianised morality the Corinthians were rated by Paul as the most gifted local church that he knew, possessing a spectacular array of Christian gifts. But somehow things were not right with them.

It was surprising that St Paul, the early church's first great theologian, was apparently unable to teach the Corinthian Christians some vital steps in Christian growth. They were, he said, still spiritually infantile and unable to digest more advanced spiritual truths; like babes they were still on a milk diet rather than solids. And strangely the evidence for this was not theological so much as relational! There was jealousy and quarrelling among them and a competitive spirit which probably came from their differing abilities to use spiritual gifts. Paul was disappointed that rather than behaving Christianly they were living 'just like ordinary men'. They were true Christians, good people, but because of relational breakdowns it was hard to see the *extra*ordinary quality that ought to have been in their lives. Except for their religious activities did they appear to be much different to their pagan neighbours?

---

1   1 Corinthians 3: 1 to 4 (RSV)

Did the Corinthians take St Paul's criticism to heart? Did they make radical changes in their life-style? Did they abandon their combative attitude to each other and the 'ordinariness' that it produced? Did they try again to be different from their pagan neighbours?

Making a difference?

It is very interesting to note how believers, throughout the ages, have tried to make themselves different to others, such as wearing different clothes and using particular forms of speech. For example, the Amish people in the United States have certainly become distinct from other Americans. In their dress and speech and in keeping to certain archaic customs they have tried to live in the modern world as they had lived in the past. They no doubt believe that in the 'good' old days things were better and people were more holy than in the present and that that original way of life must not be abandoned.

Another group of people, this time in the Old Testament, seemed to feel the same way. The descendants of Rechab, having made their way across the desert with the other Israelites, refused to become agriculturalists in the Promised Land. They were convinced that the semi-nomadic way of life in which God had led them and fed them in the past was the right way to live. The dazzling new life in Canaan with its agriculture and its cities frightened them and they wanted none of it. They drank no wine in protest against agriculture and the agricultural gods.

The dedication and the discipline of the Amish and the

Rechabites was admirable but it was clear that the major purposes of God did not go with them. In America the Amish were left behind and in Palestine so were the Rechabites, each of them only on a side-track in sacred history. Becoming God's 'peculiar people'[2] often can result in making believers odd or bizarre, religiously eccentric and irrelevant. If we are afraid to tackle the challenges of the modern world apparently God is not afraid and the attempt to make a difference does not come from shrinking from the demands of the future.

But how am I to become a good man or woman? How will it make me specifically Christian unlike 'ordinary men and women'? How can I become good without becoming odd or some kind of religious extremist? If the advice to the Corinthians tells me anything it says that my difference from others must be relational. This should not surprise since a large proportion of the ethics of the New Testament deals with how we should relate to and serve other people. Someone has said that in the nine aspects of the fruit of the Spirit in Galatians the first three tell how we relate to God, the second how we relate to others and the third how we relate to ourselves.[3] Again, it is no surprise that the very essence of Jesus' teaching in the Sermon on the Mount deals with attitudes and actions towards others.[4]

Jesus maintains that ordinary human responses which are considered 'normal' are – for his followers – just not good enough.

---

2 Deuteronomy 14:2 (KJV) The NIV translates 'treasured possession'
3 Galatians 5:22
4 Matthew 5: 46–7

He looks for something more, something *extra*ordinary by human standards but appropriate for those who follow him. He shrewdly notes that everyone, even people from the lowest strata of life, have affection for family and friends. Their love for others is exclusive and operates only in the limited circle of their affinities, whereas our love must be unconditional and indiscriminate, going beyond loving the neighbour even to loving the enemy. Such love is like God's, who makes the sun rise on good and bad alike, who sends rain on those who love him and those who do not. If we can love like that, says Jesus, we will resemble our Father in heaven and show a 'family likeness' to the watching world.

Bishop Asterius of Petra (died 365) gives a wonderful example of this in the life of an old man named Phocas who lived in Sinope in Asia Minor in the first years of the fourth century. He was a generous and hospitable man who welcomed weary travellers passing by. As a convinced Christian he was eventually placed on a Roman hit list for execution during the Diocletian persecutions. One day there came to his house executioners who were enquiring as to his whereabouts. He replied that he knew the man they sought and would lead them to him in the morning but would they not first come inside and enjoy his hospitality? They agreed and there followed a wonderful time in which they enjoyed themselves immensely and talked about their lives and their families

When they retired to bed Phocas, a keen gardener, went out into his garden to dig and to think. He knew that by morning he could be far away but he also knew that this would place the lives of his executioners in jeopardy with the authorities. So next day he told them who he was. They were horrified and tried to find some way of avoiding the execution of this good old man. But he told them he was not afraid to die because of his faith in Christ and he then informed them that they would not even have to dig his grave since he had done that himself during the night! Surely such extraordinary love eventually outlived and outlasted the hostility of the Roman Empire.

Of course such a high ideal goes way beyond even the best efforts of human nature. It leaves behind the Mrs Springers of this world and also, in a sense, even the Corinthian Christians despite what the Gospel had done for them. Although we can never attain to holiness without effort and sometimes struggle, it is impossible to attempt to do it without relying on an inner source of true goodness which we must think about now.

DISCUSSION QUESTIONS

1. What do people who claim to be 'good' mean by the term? How should we relate to this claim in a positive way?

2. What is the difference between 'works' and 'good works' in Ephesians 2: 8–10?

3. The Corinthian Christians were very gifted but were living quite 'ordinary' lives. What would be the signs of this among believers to-day?

4. How 'different' to others should we Christians be and in what way?

5. What was the 'difference' to which Jesus referred in the

Sermon on the Mount?

6. Why are relationships so important to Christian living?

2   The Inner Life

The Christian life is as attractive as it is daunting. Who would not like to live out all the beautiful qualities in the New Testament? To be forgiving, thankful at all times, gentle, patient and always motivated by love – becoming a virtual 'identikit picture' of Jesus himself. But, as Paul said about Christian ministry, 'who is equal to such a task?'

Unfortunately, when human beings are faced with an ethical challenge they have an innate tendency to turn it all into rules and regulations. The flexible guidelines the Bible gives us to guide us through life soon become rigid rules which rob us of our freedom. And this, sadly, allows the human ego to stay in charge and be master of its own affairs. The religious authorities of Jesus' day who had done this so systematically lived in such a legalistic strait-jacket that they just could not cope with the free and creative goodness that Jesus was teaching. Worse than that their legalism carried them away from the inner motivation of the heart into more external and mechanical forms of religion with the focus not on God and their neighbours but on their own efforts.

Beware of the Pharisee

So we must avoid at all costs changing the New Testament's precepts into a kind of Christianised Phariseeism. These beautiful principles are so important that we must at all costs discover how to incorporate them into our personal lifestyles but without deadly legalism. But how is this to happen? From a legal requirement *outside* of us they must become a motivating force *inside* of us. In this book we will examine how this can happen. An inadequate analogy is perhaps the way in which we teach children good manners and polite behaviour. In the beginning they do not always initially accept what adults say and – perhaps in the teen years – fight back against parental pressures and 'lectures'. The young can be untidy and selfish and sometimes rude. But as time passes and they mature, many adult ideas begin to appear rather like a photographic image slowly emerging in the dark room. It seems that our parental guidance has gradually been 'internalised' and become something that they now own for themselves as personal behaviour.

Like most illustrations this one is inadequate. The independence from a parent in the growing child is quite different from what happens when Christ – by his Spirit – enters our inner being. The Spirit's partnership with us is a continuing one and we do not outgrow the need of the Spirit and the Spirit's enabling nor does the Spirit over-ride or replace our unique personalities. As part of

God's workmanship, made in the divine image, Christ's coming into our lives actually humanises us and opens up the way for us to become our true selves and to reach our full human potential.

We can see the internalising process in Jesus' disciples. During his earthly ministry they seemed to have a great ability to misunderstand him. Peter tried to talk him out of the cross; James and John begged him to obliterate a Samaritan village for the 'crime' of not listening to him. But when, at Pentecost, the Spirit came powerfully into their lives, they began to change. They had a new courage and a clearer understanding of Jesus' true identity and a proper grasp of the significance of the cross. Paul would later say that they had become 'one spirit' with the Lord so that the Christian life is nothing more or less than Christ living in us, and Christ loving in us.[5] This we must explore in the following chapters.

DISCUSSION QUESTIONS

1. How can we learn to obey God's laws without becoming slaves to legalistic behaviour?
2. Why is such behaviour still too self-centred even when very moral?
3. Can we internalise such good principles so that they become an inner motivation?
4. How did this happen to Jesus disciples? How does it happen today?
5. What part does the Holy Spirit play in this process?

---

5   1 Corinthians 6:17 (RSV)

6. What did St Paul mean by the phrase becoming 'one spirit with the Lord'? How do we experience this?

3 The Fifth Columnist

With such rich resources for the living of the Christian life what is it that hinders our progress? Why is it that when we want to live a good (Christian) life we seem to be up against hidden forces which thwart our deep desire to be holy and Christlike? If we were to use a 'time machine' and go back to dialogue with the Corinthians we might perhaps warn them that sincere – even gifted – Christians sometimes appear too much like unconverted people and spiritual infants. We would, of course, be speaking of the fact of our fallen nature and the indwelling power of sin.

Sin is described in various ways in the Bible. It is a 'transgression' because it steps across the moral boundaries which God has set; it is 'missing the mark,' falling well short of the high standards which God has set; it is 'lawlessness' because it makes us into spiritual outlaws who flout God's standards and purposes. What each of these definitions has in common is that they are all directed against God and an indication that we have usurped God's rightful place in our lives.[6] They also remind us that behind God's laws stand divine love and behind that stands the Great Lover - God. Sin is not, then, merely an infringement of God's standards it is an onslaught on God's person and the cross of Christ is the flagrant evidence in the world's history of how humanity has tried to remove God from time and temporality.

The secret enemy

It is important for us to recognise that in rejecting God as love's source we have also rejected love's way. Instead of its sacrificial self-emptying action we have chosen the hideous abnormality of self-centredness. Like a hungry and rapacious whirlpool we have reached out to grasp and draw to ourselves all that passes of both people and possessions. And, as with a whirlpool, there is with all it has grasped, a hollow space within, an unfilled and unfillable void.

If I were still explaining this to Mrs Springer she would, by this time, be thoroughly scandalised by my commentary on the world and its inhabitants. As a 'good' person she would be horrified at my description of human nature. She would see me as some kind of misanthrope whose views on human nature were so badly distorted that they posed a danger to modern civilisation

---

6 King David, having committed adultery with Bathsheba and engineered the death of her husband, nonetheless recognised that all sin is ultimately against God – see Psalm 51:4.

and contemporary culture. That I should be teaching young people such things bodes ill for the future of the human race. So in fairness to her I would probably have to point out that our fallen nature does not mean that everybody is just as evil as it is possible to be. There are many sophisticated, educated, intelligent and perhaps charitable people who live admirable lives but who are still part of a rebel race which has decided to live independently of God. And one of the characteristics of this condition is an innate self-deception which often makes it so hard to identify and thus to acknowledge.

Let me again visit the Corinthian Christians and remind them of how important it is for them and all Christians to be aware of the same toxic principle at work in us. As new Christians they would have been taught to renounce their more blatant and flagrant sins, and even to abandon their best self-efforts so as to accept from God the righteousness which Christ has won for them on the cross. But perhaps they would not have fully appreciated the continuing subtle and devious activity of the self even at their most religious moments?

Christians, forgiven and justified, are still 'disabled' people, still engaged in the never-ending battle against sin and self-centredness. In the three traditional enemies of the Christian, in the 'trinity of evil' (the world, the flesh and the devil) it is the second one that is at work inside our defences. It is the same 'flesh' that made St Paul cry out 'what I do is not the good I want to do; no, the evil I do not want to do - this I keep on doing'.[7] The flesh,

---

7   Romans 7:15

as the English word might suggest, is not the human body. The Greeks were inclined to say that although the spirit was a pure spark come from God the body was intrinsically evil.[8] But the Bible always sees the body as part of God's good creation destined for a final transformation and which could – unlike the flesh – be offered to God as a 'living sacrifice, holy and pleasing to God'.

The flesh is a principle that operates in and through the body and the mind as an 'enemy within the camp'. The Greek word *sarx* is not easy to translate into English (as you can see from various Bible translations none of which are entirely satisfactory).[9] The *Dictionary of the New Testament* offers an excellent definition from Anthony Thistleton. He describes the flesh as 'the outlook orientated towards the self, that which pursues its own ends in self-sufficient independence from God'. Thus the sins of the flesh are not only bodily ones but also sins of the mind and spirit such as 'idolatry, witchcraft, hatred, discord, and jealousy, fits of rage, selfish ambition, dissensions, factions and envy'.[10] The flesh obviously drives all kinds of egotistic impulses to have their way. A traitorous double-crosser, it always sides with sin and the self to thwart our attempts to live Christianly but thankfully St Paul reminds us that it was crucified with Christ so as to give us the *potential* ability to break loose from its power and, with the Holy Spirit's help, shut down its treacherous activity.[11]

---

8   *Soma sema* was a Greek saying meaning 'the body is a tomb'.

9   For example 'the lower nature', 'the unspiritual nature', 'the carnal attitude', etc.

10 Galatians 5:20

11 Galatians 5: 24 & 25

The mysterious mix

Christians are sometimes bemused by this rather ambiguous situation. Forgiven and justified they wonder about the fact that they are, as Martin Luther observed, 'at the same time justified and yet a sinner'.[12] The necessity of thus living 'in two worlds' at once will be dealt with more fully in a later chapter.

We human beings are a curious mix. Part of the animal kingdom, a handful of 'dirt', as the colourful description in Genesis puts it, we are at the same time a God-breathed image of the Divine Personality. With bodies made of water and various chemicals we are akin to the beasts and yet, alone in all creation, we have the ability to communicate with God. We are where heaven and earth meet each other and the mysterious mix into which the Son of God himself eventually made his way.

Humanity was given the unique task of caring for and controlling this beautiful planet. But earth's submission to us depended entirely on our submission to God. There was a hierarchy of control that ran down from God through us to the world of nature. Within our own beings this meant that the lower animal side of us was subject to the spiritual side only so long as our human spirits were subjected to the Great Spirit of God.

Our rebellion against God therefore resulted in an enormous disruption in our human nature. Having broken the link between God and ourselves we set up a similar chain reaction of mutinies in our own being. As CS Lewis put it: 'the Enemy persuades man to rebel against God: Man, by doing so, loses power to control

---

12 *Simul Justus et peccator*

that other rebellion which the Enemy now raises in Man's organism (both physical and psychical) against Man's spirit.' The flesh, the lower side of us, now demands to supersede and control the higher. This does not mean, as we have seen, that the body and its appetites are evil in themselves. The body's desires are entirely legitimate and simply doing what they were created to do. The evil lies in the fact that because of our failure to submit to God, these desires refuse to submit to us and rebel against their lowly position. They attack and demand control, they despoil the human spirit and they mar their own nature and destiny. As wonderful servants they have become terrible masters. The flesh therefore may express itself in gross acts of sin but it can also be sophisticated, even religious – it can even quote Scripture! But strip away its disguise and it will always be the self, manoeuvring to get its own way. This is the enemy within.

DISCUSSION QUESTIONS

1. Why is sin actually against the being of God? How does the cross of Christ reveal this so flagrantly?
2. How can we explain this fact to 'good' people who have not accepted Christ?
3. In what way are Christians forgiven but still 'disabled' by sin and self-centredness?
4. Explain how the body is good although through 'the flesh' it can be used in evil ways.
5. Describe ways in which you see the 'flesh' at work in your

life or in the lives of others?

6. How does humanity's rebellion against God cause other rebellions in our nature? Give some examples.

4   Love is the Way

*I*n my search for a way to become a good man I have certainly discovered what can prevent it from happening! I have also found that even if I was a respectable, upright and law-abiding Christian, I might still lack that special quality that distinguishes me from being like an 'ordinary' person. And it seems that the missing piece of the jigsaw is, as it was for the Corinthians, a relational matter. The Christian life is not only Christ living in us, it is actually Christ *loving* in us.

Love is a word so extensively used that it is sometimes hard to define. In English this one small word carries an enormous weight, describing our commitment to God or a spouse but also desire for such mundane things as a partiality for fish and chips or chocolate flavoured ice cream. Love can be sentimental and express itself in 'warm fuzzies' and, in romantic terms it is the eternal theme of songs, novels and movies. Sadly it can also describe the illegitimate 'love affair' which leads to the abandonment of promises and obligations made to spouses and children. 'Falling in love' this way inevitably leads to 'falling out of love' with others. Such a description of love is light years away from what the Bible means by the word.

The Bible's idea of love takes us right to the heart of Christianity. Indeed, it takes us to God. The Apostle John rather daringly says that God *is* love.[13] Love also takes us to what motivated the Gospel and caused God to give his only Son to save the world[14] and it takes us to the one quality that fulfils all of God's laws.[15] The word most commonly used for 'love' by the New Testament writers is the Greek word *agape.* The Greeks, as analytical thinkers, recognised that there were different ways in which we can love. They had in mind the love of desire, the love of friendship, and the love that is found in families. Perhaps they chose *agape* from among the four because it had been used in the Greek version of the Old Testament. It has been suggested, however, that *agape* had almost been discarded by Greek thinkers and was thus open to be 're-minted' by Christians to express a new and specifically Christian meaning.[16]

---

13 1 John 4:8. It is said that Martin Luther once remarked that if we had the ability and the materials with which to paint love we would never complete the task because before the last brush stroke we would have fallen on our faces before what was in fact a portrait of God.

14 John 3:16

15 Galatians 5:14; Romans 13:8

16 Modern scholarship has, however, discovered that although the noun *agape* is only found once outside the Bible, the verb *agapao* was making something of a comeback by the fourth century BC.

Love defined

In a monumental study of two ways to love – *Agape and Eros* – Anders Nygren compares and contrasts Biblical love with *eros*, the most common Greek word for love (though not found in the New Testament). *Eros*, says Nygren, is characteristic of human love because it is 'desire, egocentric love, for which man occupies the dominant position as both starting point and goal. The starting point is human need and its goal is the satisfaction of that need'. Such love is 'ordinary' because it needs to be stimulated by attraction to something or someone desirable. But our New Testament writers saw in Christ (and especially at his crucifixion) that he was giving himself for those who were very far from being attractive, 'while we were yet sinners'.[17] They would have also recognised that human love (*eros*) needs, in some sense, to *possess* the object of its desire. By way of illustration, when applied to sexual love it describes the passionate desire to possess the attractive beloved. William Barclay, rather whimsically, says of *eros* that although it has an important part to play in life it is 'still unconverted'.

Agape or Biblical love is, in a way, the complete reverse of *eros*. It is self-giving and sacrificial, modelled on Christ himself. His self-giving was not done from a desire for personal gain but for the good and benefit of others. Love is therefore seen in action or not seen at all.[18] It is only *known* when we, like Christ, 'lay down our life' for others.[19] However, despite the radical contrast

---

17 Romans 5:8

18 1 John 3:18

19 1 John 3:16

between the two ways of loving, *agape* does not replace the other loves. Rather it moves in behind them to redeem and sweeten them and to nullify their toxic self-centredness. Sexual love, friendship and family love, without the healing power of *agape* can become very destructive. It is *agape* alone that helps each of them find their true nature by humanising all relationships.

This *extra*ordinary love, as we have seen, fulfils all God's laws since all of them – rightly understood – are really practical ways of loving God and loving other people. So Jesus, despite his many conflicts with the religious lawyers of the day, claimed that he had not come to abolish the Law but to fulfil it, setting it free from the deadening legalism with which it was observed, energising it to repair and sweeten peoples' dealings with each other. Those who opposed Jesus had obviously not seen the Law's deeper motivation and so had opted for its external 'letter'. Although they had observed the minute details of the Law and its prohibitions. they had missed the point and failed to observe its calling for 'justice, mercy and faithfulness'.[20] St Paul, as a former Pharisee, had discovered when entering the life of Christ that God's indwelling Spirit melted the stern outlines of the Law and replaced them with the free and flexible ways of love. He had seen how 'the letter kills' and also how 'the Spirit gives life' and that 'where the Spirit of the Lord is there is freedom'.[21]

We owe so much to St Paul for the way in which he dealt with all these issues and explained them so clearly. When, as a

---

20 Matthew 23:23

21 2 Corinthians 3:6; 17

missionary, he moved beyond the Jewish world into the world of the Gentiles he was able to work out a Christian ethic that applied to people of all times and all places. To Jews, prone to legalism and Gentiles, prone to licentiousness, he offered the third "L" – liberty. The love ethic did not discount the true beauty of the Law but was free and flexible, unshackled by rules and regulations, which neither permitted self-righteous legalism on the one hand or self-indulgent 'freedom' on the other.[22] Paul taught us how love approaches every culture and every time with a deeply held aim to sacrifice itself for the good of others. It has surely taught us how to be good people.

DISCUSSION QUESTIONS

1. How can we explain the fact that the Christian life is Christ *loving* in us? What does this mean?
2. How has the word 'love' been devalued by over use?
3. Why did the Apostle John say that God *is* love? What did he mean by this?
4. How is the Bible's idea of love so different to ordinary human loving? In what way is this so?
5. How does Christ's laying down his life on the cross teach us how we should love others? Give some examples.
6. How does Christian love give us liberty to live in the right way?

---

22 Galatians 5:13

5 The Great Collision

*I*t was inevitable that the self-centred activity of a flawed humanity should clash with the self-giving activity of the God who is love. Although made in God's image and designed to display divine love, we have made the fateful decision to think and act independently of God and turn in upon ourselves in the quest for self-centredness and self-realisation. We clash with God and we clash with other human egos since there is only room for one on the throne and they too compete there for pre-eminence and primacy. Such is the history of humanity, and such is much of the history of the Bible as well. God bears and forbears with men and women. God is slow to anger and of great kindness. But when, in Christ, God visits them in great humility they are still obdurate and impenitent. Even those who should have known best – the religious leaders of the day – lead the antagonism and direct the opposition to Jesus.

Consequently, in the mind of Jesus, there had to be a final

confrontation between God's way and human will. The battle that had persisted for millennia had to be brought to a conclusion. There had to be a showdown or the whole moral fabric of the universe would be in jeopardy forever. For Jesus that meant the cross as the one and only way that this impasse could be overcome and any progress made. Satan, obviously aware of this strategy, tries to tempt Jesus to go another way when he offered him three alternatives to fulfilment at the start of his public ministry. Even Peter, one of the disciples who was closest to Jesus, joined the campaign to promote alternatives to the cross. Jesus is in no doubt about Peter's allegiance at this point. Peter speaks for Satan and for fallen humanity as well because 'he does not have in mind the things of God but the things of men'.[23]

Checkmate!

The cross reveals all. It shows how self-centred humanity was bent on engineering the execution and removal of God and God's ways. But the cross also shows how divine self-giving love also reveals its true nature in all its fullness at the cross. Love used no other weapons but love's offering of itself as a sacrificial victim for the good of all (even those who personally demanded its execution). God, like a master chess player, was prepared to lose a most precious piece and, at first, appear to be the universe's greatest all-time loser. Jesus was going love's way not by force but by self-sacrifice. He was committed to the course in order to infiltrate evil's defences and dismantle them from within. The resurrection

23 Matthew 16:23

of Jesus clearly demonstrated that he had won this momentous battle not only for himself but also for us. God could now cry 'checkmate' to the devil and to humanity's stubborn rebellion. And there is more.

When Jesus went to the cross he went as representative man – the new Adam. He subsumed and offered for execution our sick and damaging egotism. He did this so that our 'self' could be crucified along with himself. This was giving us, through his Spirit, the ability to claim his conclusive dying and rising again to our own personal situation and to experience what CS Lewis described as 'transpositions of a divine theme into a minor key'.

Of course, the statement 'God is love' has always been true. It didn't just become true in the life and death of Jesus. Love was always shown and known in the Triune being that is the God whom Christians worship. This limitless capacity for love preceded the sending of Jesus to save the world or, as George Macdonald puts it, 'he (Christ) did that in the wild weather of his outlying provinces which he had done at home in glory and gladness'.[24] So the victory on Calvary's hill has given us what CS Lewis referred to as 'the Spirit of the willingly dying God' to lead us to countless personal crucifixions and individual resurrections, to a dying to self-will and a rising to new life marked by outreach to others. Leaving behind the fantasy world of self-centredness with its false promises of happiness and fulfilment, we begin to discover at last what human beings were created to be and to do. We discover the *extra*ordinary life of love.

---

24 Revelation 13:8

DISCUSSION QUESTIONS

1. Why did the religious leaders of Jesus' day oppose him more than others?

2. What was Jesus' great appeal to the various outcasts of society?

3. Can you think of places in the Bible where Satan attempted to divert Jesus from the necessity of the cross?

4. How did love win the day in Jesus' battle against sin and death on the cross?

5. How was our egotistic rebellion against God dealt with (as in crucified) on Christ's cross?

6. How does the Holy Spirit bring to us Christ's victory on the cross and apply it to our daily lives?

6   Life in Two Worlds

*C*hristians sometimes find it difficult to understand why, having been made new by God's Spirit, they still have to battle with the old enemies represented by the world, the flesh and the devil. They have entered a new age of righteousness and life which has invaded the old fallen age so they live in a kind of 'overlap' between the two. In this 'middle ground' great pressures come upon them from both ages and it is their responsibility to flee from conformity to the one and to pursue conformity with the other. It is this paradoxical situation that makes it essential for us to have the right perspective on the two ages. If we are overwhelmed with the blessedness of the new age alone so as to become blithely optimistic about living Christianly this can easily lead to a form of perfectionism which does not take sin seriously enough. If, on the other hand, we are oppressed by the dark and sinister power of the old age we can become prey to defeatism and depression. So it is essential that we recognise the power and impact of each sphere of influence but without losing our confidence in the fact that we are on the winning side and that 'the one who is in you is greater than the one who is in the world'.[25]

Now and not yet

Our life in two worlds is expressed in a number of ways in the New Testament. The Kingdom of God has come with Jesus but, as we say in the Lord's prayer, it still requires us to pray for its fullness to come. St Paul says that we have 'died' to sin but we need to 'put to death' all kinds of sinful activity. Because the old age has been invaded by the new without replacing it we are 'saved in hope'. Essentially, we are truly saved but not yet fully saved.[26] That for which we still wait is often explained in the New Testament as an *unveiling* of something which at present is still hidden. We serve an invisible King who reigns over a Kingdom which cannot be located or mapped in a physical sense. It is also unrecognised by the world. Our life too is hidden 'with Christ in God'[27] but when Christ will visibly 'appear'[28] we too shall appear with him and our inner likeness to him will be brought to the surface and be openly visible. And since we humans are the apex and crown of God's creation our unveiling will also be good news for the whole universe. It will be liberation from the bondage to

---

25 1 John 4:4

26 Romans 8:24: 'salvation' is mostly used in the future tense in the New Testament.

27 Colossians 3:3

28 The Greek word *parousia* means to 'appear' and was often used to describe Christ's return, sometimes translated as his 'coming'.

frustration that our fallenness has imposed upon it.[29] Gripped as it were by birth pangs, the creation presently labours to bring forth the new order and the creation 'groans' in anticipation of it. In concert with the groaning of God's Spirit, we share the pain associated with the arrival of a new world as we await the *grand finale* of the completely transformed order.

To understand fully our life in two worlds we must recognise what binds us to each of them. Our link with the new age is the gift of God's Spirit. Coming into our lives the Spirit has brought into the present some all-important blessings of the world to come. These blessings are also described as the 'first fruits of full salvation'.[30] We experience forgiveness and justification now. We do not have to wait till we hear the verdict of 'not guilty' in the eternal courtroom. The Spirit has also given us a new birth, a kind of spiritual resurrection, and awakened in us a love for God's word, a love for God's people and a desire to live God's way. And perhaps the sweetest gift of all, the Spirit has brought to us a sense of being the adopted children of a loving heavenly Father.[31]

The battle of the body

Our link with the old age lies in the fact that our bodies are not yet redeemed and are therefore open to the traitorous attacks of

---

29 Romans 8: 19–23

30 2 Corinthians 1:22–25; Ephesians 1:14. This phrase reflects the custom of giving a portion of a future consignment as a guarantee of the quality which was to come.

31 Romans 8:23

the flesh.[32] It was for this reason that the Son of God himself took human flesh so that he could – through his death – condemn sin in the flesh and prepare us for a resurrection like his. We are destined to resemble him and finally become 'Jesus lookalikes'.[33] If our as-yet unredeemed bodies are part of the problem, they are also part of the answer. The body, as we have seen, is never described as evil in the Bible but was, to Hebrew thinkers, something like the soul in its outward form. It is thus the agency through which the real person lives and moves and has his or her being. It is 'the very self' (as the *New English Bible* translates 'body') the actual visible down-to-earth person and thus the clear indicator of what is going on inside. If we are to be good (Christian) people then we must be so bodily as well or not at all. Pious wishes and dreams which are not 'earthed' in visible activity are spurious.

The body's 'parts' – the hands, the feet, the tongue – must be placed at God's disposal and its 'misdeeds' must, with the assistance of God's Spirit, be put to death.[34] The outward offering of the body is matched by the inner transformation of the mind by the Spirit. Mentally we are under constant pressure to conform to a godless and selfish society which has no room for God. Thankfully the Spirit renews our minds, changing our thinking habits so that we begin to discover God's will for our lives and finding that this is 'good, pleasant and perfect'.

In the first two verses of Romans 12, Paul uses 'temple'

---

32 Romans 8:23
33 1 John 3:2; Philippians 3:20–1
34 Romans 6:13; 8:13

language to describe how this happens. The offering of the body is a living sacrifice, a spiritual act of worship. Instead of the dead animals brought in the past to the temple we now bring living sacrifices to God, that is, ourselves so that we can translate ordinary everyday living into something 'holy and pleasing to God'. We no longer need an actual shrine or sanctuary in which to do this since 'divine service is rendered daily' in the office, the factory, the field, the kitchen and the schoolroom.

DISCUSSION QUESTIONS

1. How can we experience being 'on the winning side' against sin and still be aware of our fallen nature?

2. What does it mean to be 'saved in hope', that is, truly saved but not yet fully saved?

3. How is our life still 'hidden with Christ in God' and what will its eventual transformation be like?

4. What difference to our lives does our adoption into God's family make?

5. Why can our bodies be part of the problem and yet also part of the answer to Christian living?

6. What is involved in making our bodies (real selves) a 'living sacrifice' to God? Give some examples.

7   On the Move

We have been examining the overview or ground plan of the Christian life. This is important. It is almost as necessary as using a map and compass to plot a course and reach a destination. But getting the picture right intellectually is not enough. There must be discernible and measurable progress. There must be movement forward from conformity with the old age into conformity with the new. With bodies surrendered and minds renewed we must now begin to make the most of the future blessings that God's Spirit has brought to us so as to apply them to the challenges of daily living. There must be a realistic exercise of a faith which trusts in God and God's word to 'give substance to our hopes and convince us of realities we do not see'.[35] We must use faith as a God-given ability to take hold of God's promises and make them real to us now even though they are at present unseen.

35 Hebrews 11:1 (RSV)

Faith's regular companion is repentance. This 'change of mind' joins with faith in the forward movement away from the old age. It is the about-face from the negatives of the past, moving us away from self-centeredness into Christ-centred living.[36] Repentance takes us from 'the mind of the flesh' to 'the mind of Christ' and St Paul graphically illustrates this point in the second chapter of his letter to the Philippians. Pleading with his readers to abandon 'selfish ambition and vain conceit' with the necessity to 'consider others better' than themselves, St Paul introduced them to 'the attitude of mind that Christ had'.[37] Through his incarnation and crucifixion Christ showed a 'mind' of humility, self-sacrifice and costly obedience. In a series of downward steps he gave himself to human living, servanthood and a shameful death. The sacrificial mind that originated in God the Father was revealed in history by God the Son so that now, by the gift of God's Spirit, the same mind of *agape* love could be shown also in us.

Moving from the self-centred attitude to such a mind involves a radical mental adjustment. Like the prodigal son in Jesus' parable God's voice comes to us in the 'far country' of ordinary self-centred life and we 'come to our senses'.[38] We leave the old way behind and make our journey back to that for which we were created. And as repentance moves us back from the old age and its

---

36 There is amusing story of a ship's captain demanding to know why the helmsman is five degrees off course. The reply was 'coming back from being ten degrees off course, sir!' Repentance means a constant coming back from being 'off course'.

37 Philippians 2: 3–5

38 Luke 15:11f

attitudes, faith takes over and takes us forward into the blessings and behaviour of the new. They are complementary aspects of the one spiritual revolution taking us from self to Christ and from self-centredness to love.

Faith is nothing in itself but exists only because of the object in which it trusts. So there is a sense in which its 'size' is unimportant. Even faith of a 'mustard seed' dimension can cope with huge obstacles because its object, the God of heaven and earth, can cope with any eventuality. Neither is faith the feelings which are so unreliable, rising and falling according to circumstances which are either congenial or displeasing. They are 'happenstances' as someone has called them. Faith does not trust in the will-o'-the-wisp emotions but depends on (revealed) facts. In essence it exists in God and what God has promised.

Faith in the facts

Facts are essential to faith. So is truth. Faith needs that which is genuine and dependable and no amount of 'wishful thinking' will make things true if they are not true. Faith 'lets God be God' so that human beings may also be their proper selves. God is rightly seen as the Fountainhead and Source of all being and we exist entirely as recipients. St Paul's indictment in the opening chapter of his letter to the Romans is that humanity has 'suppressed' the truth that this is the only possible relationship that can exist between the Creator and the creature. We have exchanged this truth for other notions that we find more congenial to our mutinous hearts. When we receive the Gospel, it produces in us a revolutionary change of heart and mind so that we now 'honour God as God.' God's creative and redemptive power unites to bring us back from the 'far country' to the true home of the heart.

St Paul's graphic illustration of how faith works is found in the account of Abraham's trust in God in the fourth chapter of his letter to the Romans. As a former pagan Abraham began a pilgrimage basing his life on promises given to him by God. One of these promises was that in their old age Abraham and his wife would have a son. Abraham trusts God's redemptive-creative power to make this impossible thing happen. He abandons self-sufficiency and relies entirely on God who – as Creator – can 'call things that are not as though they were'. When God speaks as Creator the nonexistent must give place to the existent, the 'no-thing' must become a real fact. In Abraham's case his faith became the link between the invisible promise of God and the visible birth of his son.

We can see the same kind of thing in Jesus' healing miracles. Once again God's creative-redemptive power reached out to the bodies and minds of those who trusted Jesus to heal them. Jesus was actually calling into being a state of wholeness that did not previously exist and the link between the two mostly involved faith even of a weak and imperfect kind. The people Jesus healed had lost all hope that their paralysed limbs or blind eyes would ever be healed. Could this remarkable Jesus do something about it? Could they trust him to do the impossible?

In their healing they were introduced to a further dynamic of faith. Though Jesus was doing the impossible they discovered that they too must in a sense be involved in the miracle; a man with a withered arm must reach out his disabled arm, the paralysed man must actually rise from his bed and carry it; they must do that which had previously been impossible!

Jesus' healing miracles were an important part of his message. They illustrated powerfully how all abnormalities would be absent from the Kingdom which he had come to bring. They also testified powerfully to his divine nature. These mighty acts of physical healing spoke of God's love and compassion for the sick, the sad and the sorrowful. But Jesus had come to produce an even greater miracle than the physical by coming to cure sin-sick souls. Today we too come to him disabled by the sinister power of sin and guilt. We wonder is there any hope for us to be freed from these things. Is it possible for us to stand before God healed and forgiven? The powerful word of the Gospel calls us to be what we could otherwise never be: guiltless and justified. We too are healed just as the halt, the blind and maimed people were in the Gospels in Jesus' day.

The Christian life continues with this same dynamic of faith. With bodies surrendered and minds renewed faith must never cease to make real God's promises of victory over our selfish and sinful ways. We hear God say 'you have been set free from sin and become slaves of righteousness' and as we hold on to such truths by faith we begin to see them become real in our daily lives.[39] 'Our chains fall off, our hearts go free, we rise, go forth and follow thee' as the hymn by Charles Wesley vividly explains.

---

39 Romans 6:18

It is obvious that faith and obedience are closely connected. They are part of one and the same activity. Our believing obedience merges with God's saving activity so that his unseen promises become a visible reality. As people that Jesus healed were called upon to do the impossible, such as 'stretch out your hand', so we too, promised deliverance from our self-centred ways, can do 'the impossible' by living a new and vibrant Christian life. Such a life is, above all, a partnership in which we and God work on the same project which is making us more Christlike, helping us be the good people that God designed us to be. This partnership – as described in Philippians 2: 12b and 13 – shows clearly that we combine with God to discern the divine will for our lives. It means that we work passionately ('in fear and trembling') at living Christianly, giving our all to get the job done. While it may appear at times as if living this way is all our own work, the Bible explains that we can only succeed in living this way because God 'works in us' so as 'to act in order to fulfil his good purpose'. It is a partnership.

The adventure of faith and action is an exciting one. Faith, which Emil Brunner called 'reason healed,' has the ability to see the great future which the Spirit of God has brought into the present. It 'opens the eyes of the heart' so that we can see the 'hope to which he has called us' and turn it into a daily practical reality.[40] Like Galileo, who saw the real truth about the solar system and so revolutionised astronomical thinking, we too see things from God's point of view and act accordingly. We discover how

---

40 Ephesians 1:18

we can 'be what we are' in God's sight, despite our many human weaknesses. More and more we move forward into the heavenly blessings which have come to meet us in the midst of life. This is the *extra*ordinary life of the ordinary Christian.

DISCUSSION QUESTIONS

1. How do faith and repentance work together, each one completing the other's activity?

2. How does our fallen human nature 'suppress' the real truth about God? How can faith be called 'reason healed' (Emil Brunner)?

3. How does faith make visible things unseen? Give some examples.

4. How do Jesus' healing miracles illustrate the way faith works?

5. Why are faith and obedience to God so closely connected?

6. How does our striving to live Christianly form a partnership with God's inner working in our lives?

8 The More Excellent Way

We have covered a lot of ground since my initial conversation with Mrs Springer. I have continued to search for how to be a good man in the Biblical sense. On one hand it seemed simple: to follow Jesus and let him live out his life in me. But, on the other hand, it was a more complex matter involving him taking me to the cross with himself to replace my self-centeredness with his sacrificial love. Our quest also began by looking hard at the Corinthian Christians and wondering how people who were so gifted could be so 'ordinary' and infantile in the way they related to each other. They had been given great ability to build each other up but Paul was disappointed with the way in which they had become competitive and 'denominational' and how they showed their divisiveness by idolising great spiritual teachers such as Apollos, Peter, and even

Paul himself.[41] In St Paul's letter to the Ephesians he showed how gifted Christians could actually serve each other so as to leave behind their infantile ways and grow up into Christ.[42] He no doubt wished that the Corinthians would have been like that but it seems they needed a lesson on love.

After surveying the list of gifts found in chapter 12 of his first letter to the Corinthians, St Paul counsels them against either over-emphasising or under-emphasising what God has enabled them to do. He concludes this section by speaking of 'the most excellent way' of *agape*-love which alone will make the gifts effective. There follows a stunningly beautiful passage which spells out in detail what a really good person would be like. It seems that St Paul passes the 'white light' of love through the prism of his keen theological mind and splits it into its primary colours. It shows what love does and what it does not do in various circumstances. First, there are four examples of what happens when love is missing and then there is a variety of ways in which love works in human relationships.

First, *speech without love* is mere noise, 'sound without substance'. It has been wisely observed that the reason *why* we speak may well be more important that what we actually say. If love carries the message it will be more potent than even the most articulate advice that we might give. It will put substance into the sound but if it is lacking it will be like an empty gong.[43]

41 1 Corinthians 1:12 & 13

42 Ephesians 4: 11 to 16

43 In a modern Kiswahili New testament this is translated as 'the sound of an empty kerosene tin or a bell'.

Second, *theology without love* may appear to make someone a knowledgeable 'somebody' but in reality it leaves him or her as a theological 'nobody.' St Paul himself had a profound knowledge of the Christian faith and often urged people to gain knowledge and spiritual insight. He was certainly not an anti-intellectual. However, he knew full well that the Corinthian church's much vaunted grasp of Christian truth could 'puff' them up whereas only love could build them up.[44] No doubt he knew that arrogant theological know-alls with swelled heads and inflated egos could often look down on those who appear to be less well informed. Such an attitude can never edify or build others up.

Third, *charitable acts without love do no real good.* This may seem surprising since *agape* is a self-giving activity. But it is tragically possible for good works to be done for dubious motives. Philanthropy can be done as a grim duty or with charity's proverbial coldness. It can also be done to win God's favour or public repute or it can be done for the perverse condescending pleasure of showing largesse to others in a pathetic attempt to purchase the goodwill of needy people. Such philanthropy, says St Paul, 'gains nothing' simply because its aim is condescension by which he explains that it is done for the emotional benefit of the giver rather than for the good of the recipient. Such a whiff of selfishness in the giver often turns the looked-for gratitude into resentment and anger.

Fourth, *self-sacrifice without love* will also, surprisingly, 'gain nothing'. St Paul no doubt thinks of the personal martyrdom

---

44 1 Corinthians 8:1

that is also a subtle mode of self-centeredness. It is a self-chosen, self-driven, self-justifying commitment to a cause, a fanaticism designed to prove a self-motivated opinion. Such martyrdom can revel in opposition and persecution, wallowing in personal grievance as it makes its costly sacrifices. It can also be very manipulative by making impossible unasked-for demands on other people. In CS Lewis' book *Four Loves* there is a certain Mrs Fidget who painstakingly knits garments for her family which they do not want to wear. She slaves over the stove cooking hot meals for them when they would prefer cold ones and she sits up at night to greet them when they come home so none of them feels that they can stay out late. Mrs Fidget drives herself to 'live for others' but as Lewis suggests elsewhere you can tell who the others are by their hunted expressions! Without love all such sacrificial activity is marred by the ulterior motives in which it is done.

Fifth, true *agape* is flexible, with the ability to apply itself to a variety of situations and necessities. Above all it gives us the one and only way by which we can maintain proper relationships with each other. It shows what heals, what blesses, and what lasts the distance in our personal dealings. And although St Paul's list may seem at times well beyond our ability, we must remember that it is still what God's Spirit is striving to produce in us.

Love copes with people because it is long-suffering. Like God, love is 'slow to anger' with a great capacity to bear with people even, and especially, when they are difficult or unreasonable. Love does not retaliate against injury or insult; it hopes that there is the slightest possibility for a change of attitude in others. It is willing to wait.

Love's counterpart to patience is kindness because it is willing to do good even to those who would harm it. It has the servant spirit putting itself out to look after those who are weak, unattractive or even irritating and obnoxious. As Jesus said in the Sermon on the Mount, God is kind to the unthankful and evil and our kindness is a reflection of the divine personality.

In a fallen world it is not surprising that love, normally so positive, must also be recognised by what it does not and can not do. It does not begrudge others whatever it is they possess. Love does not resent their successes or good fortune and will do whatever it can to enrich and enhance their lives. It finds no place for 'the green eyed monster' of envy which destroys so many human relationships and erodes personal contentment.

Love spends no time talking about itself or blowing its own trumpet. It has been said that 'what moves the hearts wags the tongue' and insecure people often go into promoting their own importance. With its deep concern for others and their needs love has little time left to discuss itself.

Since love is not boastful neither is it 'puffed up' (to use Paul's word).[45] It does not allow us to engage in power-plays that ride rough shod over others in a futile attempt to be recognised as number one. When Jesus noted that his disciples were engaged in an argument about this very matter (Luke 9: 46–48) he used

---

45 One Greek lexicon defines it as being a 'wind bag'.

a little child to remind them that the only way to real greatness in God's Kingdom was to become the least in a group.

Because it is aware of the sensitivities and feelings of others love is always polite and chivalrous. It is on guard against ungracious and discourteous acts and keeps a check on how it speaks to people. Although at times it may be necessary to face some hard issues and unpalatable truths, love will always ensure that we do so in a gentle and respectful way. Love has excellent manners.

The very essence of *agape* is that, in its sacrificial self-giving, it sees itself as being there for others and not for self. This has been beautifully expressed by St Francis in his famous prayer:

> O Divine Master, grant that I may not so much seek
> to be consoled as to console, to be understood as to
> understand, to be loved as to love, for it is in giving that
> we receive; it is in pardoning that we are pardoned; it is
> in dying that we are born to eternal life.

Love with its patient, kind and gentle attitude to others does not quickly 'fly off the handle'. It is also aware of what harm can be done either by sudden uncontrolled bursts of anger or the slow 'inner burn' that warps proper judgment and prevents communication.

Love does not nurse grievances. Love has an excellent 'forgettery' and is able, like Jesus and Stephen (the first Christian martyr), to ask God not to record the harm being done to them.

Love simply erases all such things from the ledger and prevents them from continually coming up again like an unwelcome visitor.

Love is always ready to think the best of people and does not take any pleasure in hearing derogatory things about them. Love is more ready to take great pleasure especially in the truth of the Gospel that makes rejoicing in evil a fatuous exercise.

We have seen in the above facets of love what Lewis Smedes refers to as the 'limits of love'. By this he means those things that love does not do or which it prevents being done. Let me now turn to those things which it actually is and does.

Love has a remarkable staying power because it always trusts and is ever ready to make allowances for others. It does not lose faith in them or in what God can bring about in their lives. Consequently love always hopes because, although it is not a cock-eyed optimist, it does not accept failure as final. Love always perseveres and it therefore never fails (or falls or collapses) unlike all the wonderful gifts in which the Corinthians delighted. Unlike love, such gifts are for the present passing scene and will be eclipsed by eternity.

From the standpoint of eternity our earthly knowledge is partial. Although God reveals a great deal to us, God does not reveal everything and will not do so until 'the consummation' comes. St Paul's contrast of the partial with the complete is explained with the aid of an analogy: a child with his or her natural limitations does not see things that adults can see. St Paul uses the analogy based on the polished metal mirrors for which Corinth was famous. In such mirrors the vision was dull and opaque. The best that can be seen is 'darkly'. It is not unlike a riddle[46]. We may indeed live with our eyes on eternal things but our sight will be, at best, indistinct until we are 'face to face' with them. And as with seeing, so with knowing since earthly knowledge too is only partial until 'we shall know fully as we are fully known.'

If everything is partial or indistinct in our earthly journey, is there anything about which we can be certain? I would point to three things. They are mentioned frequently in the New Testament and, in one sense, form a unity. They are faith, hope and love. Notably, it is love that holds the preeminent place. Love is the essence of God's own character and the ground plan of life in eternity.

Most people want to be good. Some feel they are already good. Just as many, if not more, are not so sure. As far as the New Testament is concerned, true Biblical goodness comes on the other side of a profound spiritual revolution. It is when we hand over our human efforts, tainted as they are by a fallen nature, that we can go with Christ to the cross to be crucified and then resurrected with him into a new shape and form. We shall then find that the pattern of good in our lives takes the shape of *agape* love. Love alone can take us out of ourselves towards God and into the lives of other people in a positive manner. Love alone fulfills the essence of God's law without binding us to the shackles of legalism. Love alone is flexible enough to be relevant to all ages, all times, and all cultures. Truly love is 'the most excellent way', and the only way to be good.

---

46 *En ainigmati* from which we get our English word 'enigma'.

DISCUSSION QUESTIONS

1. *Agape* love does not replace other spiritual gifts but helps to redeem and sanctify them. How does this work out in practice? Give some examples.

2. How does a lack of love diminish the effect of otherwise excellent activities?

3. How does *agape* show itself flexible in the way it applies to different situations?

4. Why is being '*not self-seeking*' the very essence of *agape* love?

5. Why do we now see 'a poor reflection as in a mirror' and how will this contrast to our future experience?

6. Why is *agape* love an essential element for those who wish to live a good life in this world?

EPILOGUE

*I*n his uniquely imaginative way CS Lewis describes in *The Problem of Pain* how *agape*-love might be experienced in heaven:

> The golden apple of selfhood, thrown among the false gods, became an apple of discord because they scrambled for it. They did not know the first rule of the holy game, which is that every player must by all means touch the ball and then immediately pass it on. To be found with it in your hand is a fault: to cling to it, death. But when it flies to and fro among the players too swift for the eye to follow, and the Great Master Himself leads the revelry, giving Himself eternally to his creatures in the generation, and back to himself in the sacrifice, of the Word, then indeed the eternal dance 'makes heaven drowsy with its harmony'.

There is much here on which to reflect spiritually and respond to practically.